W9-CGU-301

Series
HERITAGE

No 2

ISBN 953-215-288-1

Text
NIKOLINA ĆORAK, ANA IVELJA-DALMATIN, NIKOLA ŠUBIĆ

Translator
Dr. sc. Živan Filippi

English Language Editor
Ms Celia Irving

Photos
Andrija Carli, Antonio Ćorak, Romeo Ibrišević, Zvonimir Kežić,
Branko Ostojić, Ivo Pervan, Krešo Strnad, Nikola Vilić
Arhiv Turističke naklade

Editors
Davor Nikolić, Mato Njavro, Marija Vranješ, Milan Vukelić

Editor-in-Chief
Mato Njavro

Responsible editor
Ana Ivelja-Dalmatin

Art editor
Milan Vukelić

Publishers
Turistička naklada d.o.o., Zagreb
Trgovina Anima Dubrovnik

For publisher
Marija Vranješ
Anđelko Ćorak

© Copyright by Turistička naklada d.o.o., Zagreb

Photolithographs
O-TISAK, Zagreb

Set and printed by
Vjesnik d.d., Zagreb

Zagreb, 2006.

DUBROVNIK

Pietà, a bas-relief in the lunette of the monumental portal of the church of Minor Brothers

NON BENE PRO TOTO LIBERTAS VENDITUR AURO
Freedom cannot be sold for all the gold of this world

THE STORY THAT NEVER GROWS OLD

*W*hat the Croatian writer Jure Kaštelan wrote about Dubrovnik:
If there were more Dubrovniks in the world, only one of them would be the right one: this true, authentic, unique Dubrovnik of stone-sand light. Standing on the Mediterranean sea that connects it with continents, civilizations and peoples.
Incomparable Dubrovnik.
The English writer George Bernard Shaw visited Dubrovnik in May, 1929 and became enthusiastic about the City; he sent this missive to his co-citizens:
Those who look for paradise on earth should come and see Dubrovnik.
Welcome to Dubrovnik, this City with a tradition stretching more than a thousand-years, this

Dubrovnik, romantic, unusual and exceptional

medieval City that stands at the southernmost area of the Croatian Adriatic coast. See the City-treasury of rich cultural heritage, enjoy its Mediterranean climate, its beautiful landscapes, meet its industrious and warmly hospitable people.

The sea around Dubrovnik is the cleanest in the Mediterranean, wrote Jean Jacques Cousteau in 1978, while the previous director of UNESCO, Frederic Mayor said that Dubrovnik is the treasury of the world that belongs to all of us.

In the past, Dubrovnik was a City-Republic and, like Venice, one of the best-known cultural and economic centres of the Mediterranean, and today, again like Venice, it is the best-known tourist destination in the whole of Europe.

Franciscan monastery of St Blaise, a detail of the polyptych by Lovro Dobričević, 15th C

Dubrovnik – a unique heritage ⇨

UNREACHABLE AND UNIQUE BEAUTY

"*D*ubrovnik is a small town, but is enough for the whole world", these are the words of an unknown Dubrovnik poet from the 16th century, while the entire history of Dubrovnik goes to prove it.

Dubrovnik is situated at the southern end of the Republic of Croatia, and is the seat of the Dubrovnik-Neretva County and also the centre of the tourist area of Župa dubrovačka, Konavle, Cavtat, Rijeka dubrovačka, the Dubrovnik littoral, and the islands of Lokrum, Lopud, Koločep, Šipan, Mljet, Korčula, Lastovo, the peninsula of Pelješac and the valley of the Neretva.

As a city of valuable cultural and historical monuments it has been included in UNESCO's list of the world's natural and cultural heritage. In the narrower area of Dubrovnik only, there are 1071 monuments of high category. It is host to the Dubrovnik Summer Festival, one of the oldest European festivals of drama, music and folklore established in 1950 that takes place every year from 10th July to 25th August. Dubrovnik was twice host to the world congress of PEN, in 1933 and 1993, as well as the host of numerous meetings, especially of world travel agencies (ASTA, FUAAV, DRV, SNAV…).

To the lovers of nature it offers a gentle Mediterranean landscape, to boaters various marinas and a blue limpid open sea, to the lovers of sports and recreation various facilities, and to all tourists pleasant places for rest and entertainment, and to the lovers of beauty artistic inspiration.

It is connected with the most inland centres of Europe and the world through its airport and large shipping harbour, as well as with the Adriatic coastal high road.

It is impossible just by reading and talking to know about Dubrovnik, one must see it, feel and experience it, listen to the tales told by its streets and squares, museums and galleries, houses and palaces, churches and monasteries; even the pigeons and swifts, the cypresses, walls, and its open sea tell you its tale! Dubrovnik is not only a City of history, the City of Držić, Palmotić, Getaldić, Bošković, Gundulić, and Vojnović; Dubrovnik is the City about which you dream, and the City of all times.

In daytime it attracts with its hotels and other tourist challenges, its sea and sun; at night with its music, dance, entertainment, restaurants, concerts, open-air theatres, and above all, its romantic charm.

Dubrovnik is love and beauty, eternal inspiration. It is no wonder that Ivo Vojnović, a poet of Dubrovnik asks: Will the celestial paradise be more beautiful than this paradise of mine?

⇦ *The harmony of Dubrovnik roofs and the dome of the Cathedral and the church of St Blaise*

The impressive old Dubrovnik roofs that "have outlived both people and time"

AT THE INTERSECTION OF EAST AND WEST

*T*he successful development of Dubrovnik in the past, whose economy was based on maritime and other commercial activities, was first of all helped by its favourable geographical position. It was the first harbour, protected by islands, on the maritime route from east to west, while it was well connected with the interior of the European continent along the valley of the Neretva river.

Recent archaeological investigations have proved that a settlement already existed in the area of today's City in the 6th century A.D., and most probably even before that.

It expanded after the arrival of the Croats in the 7th century A.D.

After the Byzantine rule (1205) Dubrovnik was, until 1358, under the influence of the Venetian Republic. With the treaty of Zadar it was finally liberated from its dependence on Venice, which then significantly influenced its further development. Dubrovnik came under the protection of the Croatian-Hungarian kings from 1358 to 1526. Then, after the battle of Mohač, it wisely recognized the sovereignty of the Turkish sultan under which it remained until the end of its statehood. This was due to the ever increasing Turkish policy of aggression in the Balkans, so that in 1525 the Republic of Dubrovnik decided to accept Turkish protection, with the payment of a tribute to the Turkish sultan. In return, Dubrovnik was able to continue trading along the whole of the Turkish Empire. By paying the tribute of 12,500 golden ducats, Dubrovnik protected itself successfully against the Venetian Republic, whose desire had always been to master Dubrovnik and its entire area.

During the 14th and 15th centuries, Dubrovnik had become one of the most important maritime and commercial centres in the Adriatic. The basis of this prosperity was its maritime trade. By contracting and purchasing, it extended its territory as far as Klek to the north and Sutorina to the south at the entrance to the Bay of Kotor, together with the islands of Lokrum, Koločep, Lopud, Šipan, Mljet and Lastovo.

By the 16th C the state and the legal position of the Dubrovnik Republic was completely defined. It meant that it could independently elect its rector and counsellors, forge its own coinage in the mint, hoist its flag with the figure of St. Blaise, pass independent legislature, and have its consular offices in other countries.

Then the Republic of Dubrovnik began to decline. One of the reasons for this was the discovery of America and other overseas lands when the routes of world trade crossed the Atlantic dominated by the powerful fleets of Spain, England and Portugal. Another reason was due to a tragic twist of fate. Strong earthquakes in 1520, 1637 and 1667 all but destroyed the City and its economy. Then fire devastated all that was left in the catastrophic earthquake of 1667. Many people were killed, many houses, palaces and the ancient cathedral were ruined and valuable material and cultural riches vanished without trace. One contemporary diarist wrote: Many citizens were of the opinion to leave the city for good and to erect a new settlement at Lapad. Be that as it may, only a few days after the earthquake, the noblemen of the Republic made a decision:

It has been decided that punishment commensurate with perjury should be inflicted on all who leave the soil of the Republic; we have to stay all together and work on the reconstruction of the city and contribute to its progress. This was a decision truly worthy of admiration. The City was gradually reconstructed, though it would never achieve its previous splendour.

Dubrovnik was mentioned in 1181 as a medieval commune, while its title "the Republic of Dubrovnik" went into use in the second half of the 15th century. It then stayed as republic until it was officially abolished on the 31st January 1808 by decision of the Napoleon's Marshal Marmont. Then the previous area of the Dubrovnik State was joined to other areas of Dalmatia and Austria at the Congress of Vienna in 1815. Austrian rule then lasted for some hundred years, when finally, after the first and second world wars and cessation from the Socialist Republic of Yugoslavia, Dubrovnik became an integral part of the democratic and independent Republic of Croatia.

When Dubrovnik was a commune, its citizens already had their own self-government, and in 1272 they passed a Statute with codified legal regulations that referred to internal and external political life, the economy, town planning and all other areas of their existence.

Dubrovnik as an aristocratic republic was ruled by the noblemen. All the power was concentrated in three councils – the Great Council, the Small Council and the Senate. All noblemen coming of age were members of the Great Council. From the year 1358 they elected the Rector from among themselves, and his mandate lasted only 30 days. The Rector was the

One of the Dubrovnik "little green men" who ticks time on the City bell-Tower

first among equals, and during his month of mandate he must not be "despotic".

The Republic of Dubrovnik was a neutral state that preserved its liberty by paying the tribute and by the giving of rich gifts to the rulers of the mighty powers in its surroundings. The persistence of neutrality in international relationships was thus the founding motto of the Republic of St Blaise.

Dubrovnik experienced its golden age in the 16th century, when the power and splendour of

⇦ *Minčeta, a stone crown of the City*

Venice was in decline. As a small state without a regular army the Republic of Dubrovnik still brought almost to perfection its defensive system, first by its skilful diplomacy and a widespread network of consular offices. The following buildings are outstanding in the not very big historical nucleus of Dubrovnik built according to previous plans and surrounded by city walls 1940 metres long: the Rector's Palace, the Sponza Palace, the church of St Blaise, the Cathedral, the City Bell-tower, and the Big and the Small Onofrio Fountains…A high-level standard of living in Dubrovnik is evident from the fact that it had its quarantine bases in al-

The City bell-tower, bronze hands

Dubrovnik roofs – a play of lights

A detail of the church of St Blaise: Angels – a refined beauty of stone

ready 1272, while a permanent medical service was established in 1301; its first pharmacy still works and has done continually since 1317 until the present day, being one of the oldest in Europe. In 1347, a Home for Elderly People was founded; in 1432 a home for foundlings; in 1436 the city sewage system was built; in 1438 drinking water was brought to the City through an 11,7 kilometre long aqueduct. Dubrovnik had its railway line and electric lightning in 1901, and the first tramway in 1910. Even before that, Lloyd's shipping connected Dubrovnik with Trieste, while the first modern hotel – the Grand Hotel Imperial – was opened in 1897.

FREEDOM – A SACRED THING

*T*he basic principle of the centuries-long survival of Dubrovnik and the main driving force of this City-State can be reduced only to one word – Freedom. This was the power, the strength, and the warrant of success of this City and its inhabitants. Freedom to them was a sacred factor. Ivan Gundulić, a famous poet of Dubrovnik, the poet of freedom, wrote these beautiful verses:

Oh beautiful, dear, sweet Freedom,
The gift in which the god above hath given us
all blessings,
Oh true cause of all our glory,
Only adornment of this Grove,
All silver, all gold, all men's lives
Could not purchase thy pure beauty!

Above the entrance to Fort Lovrijenac there is an inscription in Latin: Non bene pro toto libertas venditur auro – (Freedom cannot be sold for all the gold in the world). There is another inscription above the door of the City Hall in the Rector's Palace: Obliti privatorum publica curate – (Forget private worries and deal with state affairs). This meant that the public good should be put above any personal one.

Dubrovnik today is a significant cultural and tourist centre of Croatia, a white City "of stone and dreams", where "every stone has its historical significance, every wall its own wisdom."

Dubrovnik has always known how to defend its freedom both in the past and in the recent Homeland War of 1991. In the attacks of Serbian and Montenegrin aggressors the City suffered heavily, and it experienced the most devastating attack on December 6, 1991. However, having endured all this it today welcomes many visitors in an even more beautiful form. In Dubrovnik man has found his own measure and the measure its own model.

Monument to Ivan Gundulić, the poet of the Hymn to Liberty

⇦ *Atrium of the Rector's Palace – an area of perfect acoustics*

The City lies in front of us

The mighty St John's Fort illuminated by sunshine

Aquarium

MARITIME AFFAIRS AND TRADE

*T*he old men of Dubrovnik used to say, not in vain: Put your finger into the sea and yours is the whole world. Dubrovnik lived off the sea and for the sea. Its seamen and ships with the white flag of St Blaise were well-known not only in all the harbours of the Mediterranean, but also all over the then known world. Reliable sources about the existence of Dubrovnik ships in the years of 869, 1033, 1146 point to a modest beginning even before then. Dubrovnik first made trade contracts with neighbouring towns, and in the 13th century there were many of them. In fact Dubrovnik's maritime affairs and trade were at a quite high level. Dubrovnik ships were carrying the most important cargoes of the then maritime trade on the most significant international maritime trade routes. Maritime affairs experienced a strong growth in the 15th century, and their development reached its peak in the 16th century. At that time the Republic of Dubrovnik had about 300 ships and 5000 seamen from all areas of the Republic. Riches was accumulated in the City and its surroundings, while seamen and tradesmen built beautiful mansions and summer residences, and many obtained the world fame. A special place belongs to a man from the island of Lopud, Miho Pracat. He was a rich shipowner and banker who after his death left all his enormous fortune to the Republic. His monument is in the atrium of the Rector's Palace erected in 1638 as the only plebeian to deserve such an honour.

The middle of the 16th century, saw Dubrovnik at its highest height, but its maritime affairs began to decline. In 1667 Dubrovnik was struck by a great earthquake that devastated life in the Republic, and also affected badly its maritime affairs. Then in the 18th century, Dubrovnik shipping experienced a heavy crises from which it recovered rather slowly. The last and heaviest blow came in 1808 with the abolition of the Republic.

In spite of everything, Dubrovnik was during several centuries at the very top of maritime and trade activities.

Not only that, but the men of Dubrovnik also had a well developed trade with the countries in mainland Europe.

The shipowner Miho Pracat, the only non-aristocrat to whom the monument is erected in the Atrium of the Rector's Palace

CULTURAL HERITAGE

The City Walls – a true symbol of the freedom of Dubrovnik

The medieval city walls are surely the most telling symbol of Dubrovnik's freedom, its pride and defence through the ages. They were built, reinforced and increased between the 13th to the 17th centuries. One thousand nine hundred and forty metres of stone walling including towers, forts, bastions, and embrasures encompass the City and have been preserved until the present day thanks to the skill of local and foreign builders, but also due to that successful diplomacy in knowing how to ward off danger even when it reached the very city itself. The huge wall on the mainland side was 4 to 6 metres thick, and, on the sea side, 1 to 3 metres, while the height in some places even reached 25 metres. Four gates led into the City, two from the land and two sea gates near the city harbour. Four towers were built at the extremities. To the northwest, facing the land, the round monumental Minčeta Tower dominates the City, and is the most beautiful. It was built in the 15th century following the drawings of the builder Michelozzi, while its final appearance was enhanced by the Master builder Juraj Dalmatinac.

⇦ *City walls guard the City*

The City in the protecting embrace of firm walls ⇨

The round dominating Minčeta – a true symbol of Dubrovnik

Salute to the City

Under the watchful eye of St Blaise

The Maritime Museum bears witness to the glorious Dubrovnik maritime tradition

To the east, there is the mighty independent tower of Revelin, also the 15th century. It was built there to defend the Ploče Gate and the City harbour and was built to the plans of Antonio Ferramolino. The well-known smelter Ivan Rabljanin used ovens placed in the vast interior of this tower for casting guns and bells. The Revelin Tower was also the place from which the Dubrovnik's tribute for freedom was sent - ducats for the Sultan. On the top of the tower lies the largest terrace in Dubrovnik, an exceptional scenic area.

To the southeast side of the City, towards the sea, there is the tower of St John from the 16th century. This acted as the main defence of the city harbour and the Arsenal where ships were built and repaired, and from where the strongly built Dubrovnik ships would leave for distant world seas and continents. It now houses the Maritime Museum which illustrates the historical development of Dubrovnik's maritime affairs and also an Aquarium with 27 pools for various fish, sponges, corals, snails, octopuses, and also the sea-horse - a special emblem of the Aquarium.

The southern side of the city walls was built on the steep natural rocks facing the open sea.

To the west, there is the tower of Bokar that was begun in 1461. This defended the western entrance to the City and was designed by Michelozzi, the architect from Florence. Opposite Bokar, the impressive tower of Lovrijenac was

⇦ *Lovrijenac, the most beautiful summer stage*

A part of the mighty Fort Revelin

built on rock 37 metres high. It was used for various purposes during its interesting history: as a barracks, prison, and a storehouse, while today it provides the most beautiful stage of the Dubrovnik Summer Festival. This is a unique natural stage for the performance of Shakespeare's dramas; Hamlet's bitterness has nowhere else such an original atmosphere as on the walls of Lovrijenac. This stone giant resting between sky and earth also has its own might and soul, its defeats and victories, its secrets and longings. There is an inscription above the entrance to this tower: Non bene pro toto libertas venditur auro – Freedom cannot be sold for all the gold of this world.

"I am not the City only, I am the house of life" ⇨

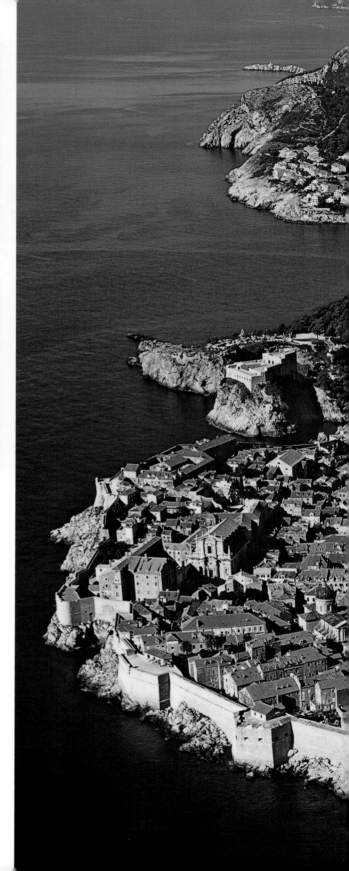

It is, indeed, an unforgettable experience to walk along the top of Dubrovnik's city walls and see the City "as if on the palm of a hand".

Pile Gate

Pile, meaning the Gate, is on the western side of the City where, in the 19th century a modern walking area led to the sea outside the walled City. From Pile, one can enjoy viewing a part of the city walls and the tower of Lovrijenac. A double gate leads into the old City above which

The blessing of the celestial protector, Saint Blaise

⇦ *The Pile Gate – encounter with the City*

Amerling's Founatin at the Pile, the work of Ivan Rendić

there is a sculpture of St Blaise. A stone bridge then takes you to the first gate under the semi-circular Renaissance tower, continuing over a wooden drawbridge that could to be raised at night and thus close off the entrance to the City. Passing through the Gothic arch of the interior gate and under the statue of St Blaise, one arrives at the Plaza, the main city street. The emblem of Pile is Amerling's Fountain, the work of the sculptor Ivan Rendić, dating from 1900. It is chiselled from firm greyish limestone mar-

The Stradun – the most beautiful Dubrovnik street

"The most distant town of Croatia, or the first, depending from which side you arrive."

ble from Carrare and depicts pastoral scenes from Gundulić's "Dubravka".

Plaza

The Plaza or, in local terms, the popular Stradun is 292 metres long. It is the pride of the City's men and women and has been described in many poems. As the poet Luko Paljetak says, Stradun is a unique street in the world in which one cannot hear the steps but only see them!

A uniform row of Baroque houses with an area for shops on the ground-floor was built after the earthquake of 1667. Stradun is still the centre of events in Dubrovnik life.

The Large Onofrio Fountain

This picturesque fountain is situated at the very beginning of Stradun and it is the work of Onofrio de la Cava in the 15th century, an architect from Naples. Round the impressive

The Big Onofrio's Fountain decorated with 16 "maskeroni" from whose mouth drinking water flows

The convent of St Clare where respected ladies of Dubrovnik passed their solitary life

carved centre there are sixteen little fountain jets of water for everyone to use – to drink, to cool their hands and to splash their faces. In the Midddle Ages anyone arriving from inland was required to wash hands and feet in this fountain as a precaution against disease.

Church of St Saviour

Opposite Onofrio Fountain, next to the main entrance up to the city walls, there is the votive church of St Saviour built in 1520 as a sign of thankfulness from the City for surviving the earthquake. It remained undamaged in the event of the great earthquake of 1667. This pearl of the Renaissance style is the work of the Dalmatian builders, the brothers Andrijić, from the island of Korčula. On the high altar can be seen the painting "Christ's Resurrection" by Pier Antonio Palmerini from 1527.

The Convent of St Claire

Behind the Large Onofrio Fountain there is the convent of St Claire, the best known of eight convents in Dubrovnik, where daughters of Dubrovnik noblemen used to commit themselves. It was built during the 13th and 14th centuries. In the 13th century it already housed foundlings, and in 1432 the Dubrovnik authorities founded here a permanent Home for Foundlings, one of the first in Europe.

The Franciscan Monastery of Minor Brothers, a precious cultural and artistic object ⇨

⇦ *The rich interior of the Franciscan church of Minor Brothers*

⇦ ⇦ *The church of Minor Brothers, Portal of brothers Petrović, 1498*

The Franciscan Monastery of the Minor Brothers

This huge complex, one of the most important buildings in Dubrovnik was the work of local masters. The monumental Romanesque-Gothic cloisters were built by Mihoje Brajkov from Bar. These cloisters are divided into four equal and symmetrical parts. There are 60 varied but harmonising capitals. These are a good example of the Romanesque tradition and depict fantastic animals with a Gothic element of human heads. In the middle of the cloisters

⇐ *The Romanesque and Gothic cloisters of the Franciscan Monastery*

A detail from the cloisters of the Franciscan Monastery

The library in the Franciscan Monastery holds the invaluable literary riches

there is a Gothic fountain from the 15th century. The monastery experienced several periods of rebuilding during its time, especially after the earthquake of 1667. The church of the Minor Brothers was burnt out completely during that earthquake. Only the Pietà on the facade of the church was preserved. It is the work of the brothers Petrović from the 15th century. The coat of arms of the great Dubrovnik poet, Ivan Gundulić, can be seen in the church.

Concerts of classical music and various recitals are today performed in the cloisters.

Pharmacy and library – special values. Of special value is the monastery pharmacy which

⇐ *The fountain with the statute of St Francis in the cloisters garden, 15th C*

Illuminated manuscript from the library of Minor Brothers

A double capital with the presentation of human figures in the cloisters of the Franciscan Monastery

was founded in 1317. It is one of the oldest pharmacies in Europe and has worked continually up to the present day within the monastery. The museum exhibits items of the old pharmacy, manuscripts and recipes in Latin and Italian. Especially interesting is the book "Indices of plants" in Latin and later translated into Croatian, which is a precious contribution to the Croatian language.

The library, holding about 70,000 manuscripts and printed books is of special cultural value. Also, the Musical Archives with 13,000 items among which there is a series of world unique items and original works. Among some 2,000 manuscripts and 206 incunabula, there are some very olds parchment sheets from the 11th century and beautifully illuminated liturgical books from the 15th C, also the calendar of saints from the 16th C, as well as the oldest transcript of Gundulić's epic "Osman" from 1653,

*The old pharmacy-museum, the Monastery of ⇨
Minor Brothers*

"Ecce homo", Francesco Francia, 15ᵗʰ C in the Museum of the Franciscan Monastery

"Ecce homo", an unknown author, 15th C, in the Museum of the Franciscan Monastery

copied by Nikola Obmučević. The only edition of "Judita" from 1521 by Marko Marulić is also kept in the library.

The Museum is situated in the Renaissance hall and is entered through the cloisters. It holds the inventory of the old pharmacy, precious goldsmith's artefacts from the Dubrovnik workshops, old vestments of the Mass, and various paintings by Dubrovnik, Italian and Dutch masters from the 16th to the 18th centuries.

The Street of Prijeko

One of the most beautiful Dubrovnik streets runs parallel with the Plaza. It is cut by a regular pattern of 14 steep streets leading up in steps from the Plaza. A row of houses with picturesque doorways, balconies and attractive windows extends along Prijeko, with a unique ambiance provided by restaurants and taverns with their rich gastronomic fragrances that line the street.

The Church of Our Lady of Sigurata

At the beginning of Prijeko, in a street called Sigurata, a convent was founded in the 13th century inside which there is one of the oldest pre-Romanesque one-aisled small churches dating from the 11th C. The convent museum holds a collection of paintings from the 16th to the 19th centuries, church plates, monstrances, a processional cross from the 14th C, two hand looms from the 14th C, lace and embroideries.

Gate of Buža

Arriving along the steep street of Ruđer Bošković from the Plaza on gets to the gate way that was opened in 1907. This bears the name of

The Gate of Buža, entrance to the City from the north

the great 18th C Dubrovnik scientist, physicist, astronomer and poet from the 18th C who was born in one of its houses.

Synagogue

The Jewish community lived in the Žudioska street at the time of the Dubrovnik Republic. They came from Spain at the end of the 15th

The Dubrovnik synagogue, one of the oldest in Europe

century and at the beginning of the 16th. Their Synagogue was founded in the first half of the 16th century and is one of the oldest in Europe. Valuable ceremonial objects of the Jewish religion have been preserved there.

Church of St Nicholas

The church of St Nicholas lies at the very end of the street of Prijeko and is one of the oldest pre-Romanesque Dubrovnik churches dating from the 11th C.

Dominican Monastery

The Dominican Monastery is also known as the monastery of the white friars. The building was begun in 1301 at the most vulnerable eastern side of the City so that this building could also be used for defence. Over the years it was surrounded by the city walls. The monastery was built by both local and foreign masters between the 14th and the 16th centuries. The façade and the south part of the church were destroyed

The small church of St Nicolas at Prijeko from the 11th C ⇨

The Dominican church, the large painted crucifixion by Paolo Venetiano, a work of enchanting beauty

⇦ *The Dominican Monastery is harmoniously inserted within the city walls*

in the earthquake of 1667 and afterwards reno-vated in Baroque style with only the south Ro-manesque-Gothic portal preserved, and was completed by the master builder Bonino from Milan. The Gothic sacristy was built by the Du-brovnik master Paskoje Miličević.

Cloisters and Museum of the Dominican Monastery

These cloisters were built in 1456 by local builders as one of the most luxurious creations of Dalmatian late Gothic style. Venetian late Gothic forms have been harmoniously inte-

The portal on the south façade of the Dominican church from the 15th C ⇨

Our Lady with saints, 15ᵗʰ C, the work of Nikola Božidarević

⇐ *The stone lace in the cloisters of the Dominican Monastery*

The polyptych "Christ's Baptism", the work by Lovro Dobričević from 1448

Triptych, the work of Mihajlo Hamzić, 1512

grated with the first signs of the Renaissance period. Arcades surround a square courtyard and also a spacious terrace. In the middle of the courtyard there is a fountain from 1559.

In the eastern wing of the monastery, a museum has been arranged with valuable altar paintings, polyptychs and triptychs, the work of the Dubrovnik painters Lovro Dobričević from the 15th C., Mihajlo Hamzić and Nikola Božidarević from the 16th C. There is also a crucifixion by Paolo Veneziano from the 14th C, a painting with the scene of St Magdalene

"Annunciation", the work of Nikola Božidarević

Museum of the Dominican Monastery: Triptych, the work of Nikola Božidarević, 16ᵗʰ C ⇨

The Dominican church, altar painting, St Magdalene, Titian, 16th

The Dominican church, altar painting "The Miracle of St Dominic, the work of Vlaho Bukovac

The Pile Gate, the eastern land entrance to the City

by Tiziano Vicelli, a triptych by Franjo Matijin from the 16th C, various works from the Flemish workshop from the 15th C, and also church plates, reliquaries and precious examples of Dubrovnik jewellery. A library holds 239 incunabula and valuable manuscripts.

Ploče Gate

This is the well fortified eastern entrance to the City consisting of exterior and interior gateways from the 15th C with stone bridges. Above the interior gateway the tower of Asimon rises as part of the city walls, while the external gate also has a wooden drawbridge which was raised at night. A stone statue of St Blaise can be seen above the Gate.

Luža and City Bell-tower

The way from Ploče on the eastern side of the city to the Plaza passes through the Gate of the

⇦ *The richly decorated well in the courtyard of the Dominican Monastery*

The Small Onofrio's Fountain from 1438

The atrium of the Sponza Palace, the most beautiful Dubrovnik palace

Customs. Above the gateway there is the old church-tower of Luža from the 15th C, while the City Bell-tower and clock from 1444 is next to it. The master smelter Ivan Rabljanin cast the big bell in 1506, and at the same time the famous bronze green men ("zelenci") (Maro and Baro) were created; their clappers ticked the hours. The bell-tower was renovated in 1929, while the original "zelenci" are now kept in the atrium of the Sponza Palace and have been replaced with copies. The building of the Main Guard – the apartment of the admiral from the 15th century is situated next to the City Bell-tower.

Small Onofrio Fountain

The fountain is situated not far from the City Clock and is a significant work of Gothic figurative and decorative ornamental sculpture. It is believed that the idea came from Onofrio de la Cava, but actually was built by the Italian sculptor Pietro di Martino of Milan.

Sponza Palace

This Gothic-Renaissance palace was built in 1520 according to a plan made by Paskoje Miličević, while most of the masonry was carried out by the brothers Andrijić from Korčula.

⇦ *The elegant Sponza Palace, during the Republic a trade centre*

The Stradun, a purple charm

The Town Hall, the administrative centre of the City of Dubrovnik

The Customs house was situated there and hence its title of Divona. On the ground-floor there were offices for estimating goods and stores, and also the mint, while a hall used for meetings and by literary academia was on the first floor.

Historical Archives of Dubrovnik

The archives of Dubrovnik are held today in the Sponza Palace as a very precious collection with rich archival material and valuable historical documents. Called the republic of papers, with the oldest documents date from one thousand and twenty two. Numerous documents held here are written in Latin, Italian, Croatian, Spanish, Turkish, Arab and other languages. Also very important is the collection of legal books, the most outstanding of which are the Statute of the City dated 1272 and the Customs Statute of 1277.

The Town Hall

Between the City Guard and the Rector's Palace there was the palace of the Great Council built in the 16th C. A large store house leant against for the storage of goods and corn. In 1816, the palace was burnt down so that a new Town Hall was built in 1882. Today, it houses the official offices of the City of Dubrovnik, the City Café, and the Marin Držić Theatre.

Orlando's Column

In the middle of the Luža Square there is Orlando's Column depicting the figure in stone of a medieval knight. It was erected in 1418 as one of the masterpieces of sculptor Bonino. A young warrior holds a shield in his left hand and in his raised right hand a metal sword. The measure of the official Dubrovnik "elbow" or "lakat" (51,2 cm) is still visible at the foot of

Orlando's Column, a symbol of independence and freedom and also the protector of trade

The church of St Blaise, the saint-protector of Dubrovnik from the distant 10th C

the column. Orlando's Column is also a symbol reminding everyone of the independence and freedom of Dubrovnik. It was the place where various decisions used to be proclaimed, public festivals announced and heavy penalties pronounced. Since 1950, the festival flag bearing the inscription Libertas has been hoisted every 10th July at the solemn opening of the Dubrovnik Festival.

Church of St Blaise

This Romanesque church of the saint protector of Dubrovnik was built in the 14th century. It survived the great earthquake of 1667 but was burnt down in the conflagration in 1706. A year later, the corner stone of the present church was laid down. The building was completed and consecrated in 1715. It was built by the Venetian master Marino Gropelli in flowery Baroque style with a luxurious portal and a wide staircase. The church keeps in its treasury the silver gilt statue of St Blaise from the 15th C. The saint-protector holds in his hand the actual scale-model of the City as it was before the earthquake of 1667. St Blaise is not only the divine protector of the City, he also stands as the synthesis and ideal image of Dubrovnik. The people of Dubrovnik have always honoured him. They devoted their church

The Baroque interior of the church of St Blaise ⇨

The silver gilt statute of St Blaise with a faithful scale model of the City on his palm

The feast of St Blaise is traditionally celebrated every year on the 3rd of February, when the City and its surroundings come to visit the saint.

The Rector's Palace, the most important building at the time of the Republic, the seat of local government and the Rector

to him, carved statues of him (27 of them have been preserved), and put his figure on the Dubrovnik flag, and on arms and coins. The Festival of St Blaise has been celebrated on February 3rd since ancient times.

Rector's Palace

This beautiful Gothic-Renaissance Palace of the 15th C was the seat of local government and its authorities for the Republic of Dubrovnik. It is one of the most important examples of secular architecture. It was twice damaged by a gunpowder explosion. After the first explosion in 1435, it was renovated by Onofrio de la Cava, while the capitals were made by Pi-

etro di Martino, After the second explosion of 1463, two well-known builders worked on its reconstruction, Juraj Dalmatinac and Michellozo from Florence. The Rector always lived in the Palace during his one-month mandate. In the Palace were halls for the Small Council and the Senate, an apartment for the Rector, a courtroom, an office, a public notary room, a prison, an armoury and a storage area. Above the entrance door of the hall for the Great Council the following inscription has been preserved: OBLITI PRIVATORUM PUBLICA CURATE (Forget private worries and deal with state affairs). It was simple and clear: public good had

The Rector's Palace, "Christ's Baptism" the work of Mihajlo Hamzić

The Rector's Palace, the study of the Dubrovnik Rector

A capital in the Rector's Palace depicting god Aesculapius in his laboratory of alchemy

to be above any personal one, which was one of the basic principles of the Dubrovnik state. The most beautiful room of the Palace are the rococo hall of Louis XVI, the Rector's study, the music hall with Marmont's clock and the Rector's bedroom. Paintings by Italian and local masters, the numismatic collection of the Republic of Dubrovnik, a collection of arms, and items from the pharmacy "Domus Christi" are there. There are also 15th C, medals, seals and the coat

The portico of the Rector's Palace, the centuries-old Dubrovnik history is interwoven in this refined beauty of stone

The stone verticals of the Rector's Palace

The atrium of the Rector's Palace, a unique concert hall

of arms of Dubrovnik's aristocratic families. The bust of the rich merchant and sponsor Miho Pracat was set in the atrium on the decision of the Senate in 1638. This rich shipowner from the island of Lopud left all his enormous for-tune to the state which then erected this monu-ment to him as the only plebeian. The atrium of the Rector's Palace is a unique area for concerts of classical music, especially during the time of the Dubrovnik Summer Festival.

Cathedral

Today's cathedral of Mary's Assumption was designed in Roman Baroque style by the architect Buffalini from Urbino in 1713. It was built on the same place as the Romanesque cathedral which was destroyed in the earthquake of 1667, while, even before that, there had been a large pre-Romanesque cathedral from the 11ᵗʰ C. Old Dubrovnik chroniclers wrote that it had been built with the money from the English King Richard Coeur de Lion who survived shipwreck not far from the island of Lokrum after his return from the Third Crusade in 1192. He took a vow that he would build a church if he escaped with his life. The cathedral was begun to be built in the 12ᵗʰ C, and was completed in the middle of the 16ᵗʰ C.

The Treasury of the Cathedral, ⇨
the coat-of-arms of the
Dubrovnik Republic on the foot
reliquary of St Blaise, 1684

The interior of the three-aisled Dubrovnik Cathedral with the view to the organs

⇦ *The Cathedral of Assumption, a very precious example of Dubrovnik art*

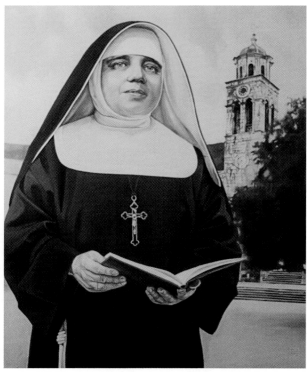

The Cathedral, the Blessed Marija Petković of the Crucified Jesus, the founder of the Society of the Daughters of Mercy

The invaluable Titian's painting "Mary's Assumption" is placed in the Cathedral

The Treasury of the Cathedral, Our Lady with the Child (Madonna della Seggiola), attributed to Raphael, 16ᵗʰ C

The cathedral treasury keeps priceless riches – reliquaries of St Blaise, gold and silver reliquaries, crosses, church plate, reliquaries of the Wood of the Cross from Jerusalem and paintings by Italian, Flemish and local masters.

The marble beauty in the interior of the Cathedral

The Treasury of the Cathedral

Our Lady with the Child, 13th C, a painting on board from the church of St Andrew at Pile

The reliquary of the hand of St Blaise from the 12th C

The reliquary of the head of St Andrew the Apostle from the 12th C

The Treasury of the Cathedral, the reliquary of the head of St Blaise, a valuable work of Dubrovnik goldsmith art

The contact of the secular and the profane ⇨

The old city port; the sea as destiny

City Harbour

One of the earliest parts of the City was formed around a late-Gothic castle near the sea, in the area of the cathedral and, later, the Rector's Palace completing thus the city harbour. The local master Paskoje Miličević was responsible, among a large number of other projects, for conceiving and buildng the harbour. Three arches of the Big Arsenal dominate it. In the Great Arsenal there was the oldest shipyard, and also large ships were also repaired there. To the east of the Great Arsenal, there is the Fishmarket Gate built in 1381, and to the west the Gate od Ponte from 1746 from which a city wall from the same period leads to the Fortress of St John, next to which the romantic Porporela was built in 1873. The huge breakwater Kaše protected the port not only from the southeast winds and seas, but also from enemies.

Gundulić's Field

From the old city harbour one rises to an area towards which the City first extended - Pustijerna. Here stands the Baroque church of Our Lady of Carmen from the 17th C, the Gothic Ranjina Palace from the 15th C, and the Renaissance Skočibuha Palace, also from the 16th C. Behind the Cathedral, across Bunić's Field lies Gundulić's Field with the monument to that great poet of Dubrovnik, Ivan Gundulić. This is the work of the sculptor Ivan Rendić from 1893. On the pedestal of the monument there are four

The vividness of the Dubrovnik market place below the monument to the famous poet Ivan Gundulić

bas-reliefs depicting four key episodes from "Osman" the best-known of Gundulić's works.

Today, Gundulić's Field is a picturesque market place during the morning while, in the evening, it is transformed into a unique stage during the Dubrovnik Summer Festival .

The Jesuits' Church

The Baroque staircase designed by the architect from Rome, Pietro Passalacqua, in 1738 fits well into the area and leads from Gundulić's Field to Ruđer Bošković's Field. The Baroque Jesuits' church of St Ignatius was built between 1658 and 1725 according to a plan of the architect Ignacije Pozza. The apse was painted by Gaetano Garcia. Next to the church there is the building of the famous Dubrovnik school Collegium Ragusinum. The library holds more than 10,000 volumes with valuable manuscripts by Dubrovnik writers and incunabula.

Granary Rupe

The Dubrovnik authorities at the time always took care to provide a quantity of corn for the city population each year in case of bad harvests or siege. The corn was stored in silos in the Granary Rupe built in the 16th C. It had 15 large silos with a capacity of 150 wagons of corn in grain. Today, it is the Ethnographic Museum showing the traditional economy of the Dubrovnik region and also its rural architecture, folk costumes and handmade textiles.

The Baroque staircase "Uz jezuite" (By the Jesuits) from 1738

The interior of the Baroque Jesuitic church of St Ignatius ⇨

The church of St Ignatius, the work of the Milan architect and painter Andrea Pozzo

The Rupe granary with its 15 dry well where the reserves of cereals were kept at the time of the Republic

Marin Držić's Home

From the Granary Rupe to Široka ulica (the widest street in another part of the City) one walks along the street of Domino. This street lies vertically to the Plaza. It passes next to the church of All Saints (Domino) from the 17th C with the some small remains from the 11th C. Next to this church is the house in which the Dubrovnik and Croatian Renaissance comic writer, Marin Držić, lived. Today, it is a memorial museum to Marin Držić. Not far from here, in the street Za Rokom there is another beautiful Renaissance church from the 16th C where somebody, disturbed by children's play, engraved by hand an inscription: Pax vobis mementomori qol ludetis pailla (Peace with you, remember that you will die, you that play with the ball).

Ploče – Eastern Part of the City Lazareti

Epidemics of contagious diseases (such as the fatal plague) were very dangerous for medieval Dubrovnik. As a model city with regard to town planning, social, economical, political,

The interior Ploče Gate ⇨

cultural and health organizations, it introduced the first quarantine against the "black death" in 1377. All persons and goods from infected areas were required to pass 30 days in isolation on the islands of Mrkan, Bobara and Supetar in front of the bay of Cavtat. The accommodation for people and the storage of goods required adequate buildingd called Lazareti.

The Dubrovnik beach called Banje

⇐ *Dubrovnik is expecting you*

The Lazareti at Ploče were built in the 17th C and they had eight buildings and five courtyards with spacious storage for goods and cattle, as well as premises for merchants and passengers.

Bete's Cave

This is situated on the road towards sv. Jakov below the old house that belonged to the aristocratic family of Getaldić. The owner of the house and cave was Marin Getaldić, called Bete, a great mathematician and physicist who performed experiments in the cave with parabolic mirrors made for destroying metal, not only lead but also silver at great distances. Today, Bete's Cave is a favourite place for numerous swimmers the majority of whom do not know much about this great scientist who was a devil in mathematics and an angel at heart.

Monastery of St Jacob

This is one of the rare monasteries outside the city walls in the area of Ploče. It was built in the 13th C in an attracted sheltered area surrounded by vineyards, cypresses and pine trees. Many learned Benedictines lived and worked there. Emissaries for paying tribute ("harač") also stayed there and prepared themselves for departure to Constantinople.

Pile – Western Part of the City

Church of St Mary at Dance

From the park of Gradac, with a magnificent view of the impressive Lovrijenac, one goes down towards the sea to Dance where there is the small church of St Mary from the 15th C. Dubrovnikan documents mention Dance as a "la-

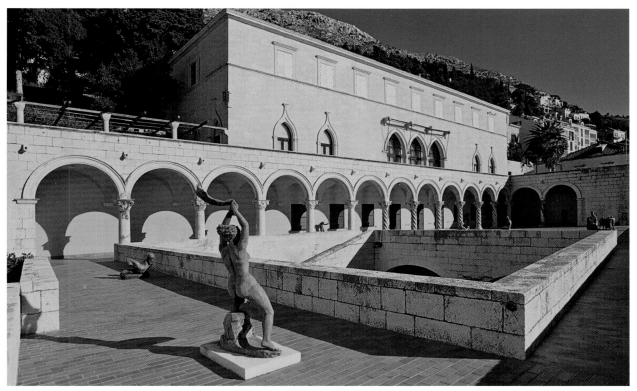

The Art Gallery holds valuable artefacts

Vlaho Bukovac, Selfortrait and the portrait of his wife, 1914

Mato Celestin Medović, A Pelješac Landscape, 1914/1915

The old Benedictine Monastery of St Jacob at Višnjica

Ploče, the eastern part of the City, an area of renown hotels and the most beautiful vistas to the old City

The largest Dubrovnik terrace and the spacious area of the Fort Revelin

Pile, the busiest art of the City

⇦ *The splendour of the Dubrovnik Stradun, our "Versailles Hall"*

The luxurious "Hilton Imperial" hotel at Pile

zaret", the last refuge for those infected with the plague. Today it houses the most beautiful Dubrovnik paintings: the altar polyptych by Lovro Dobričević from 1465 and the triptych "Our Lady with the Saints" by Nikola Božidarević from 1517, which was the last work of this outstanding artist.

Srđ

Mount Srđ is a natural protector of the City above which it rises to 413 metres. In 1810, Napoleon had the monumental Fortress Imperial built on the top, while the big stone cross was erected at the beginning of the 20th C. A beautiful view of the City, its surroundings and the open sea extends from the top. During the Homeland War Srđ was an important point for the defence of Dubrovnik, so the stone cross was hit by enemy shelling, but was rebuilt after the war.

Gruž and Lapad

Gruž lies further towards the west of the city in a protected bay. It was earlier an area with beautiful summer houses and arranged pathways of trees and flowers, of which some have been preserved, while today it is a busy settlement and commercial harbour where all major maritime and bus traffic takes place.

Lapad is situated opposite Gruž at the foot of the picturesque hill of Petka. This is a settlement of family houses, hotels and other

The church and the convent of St Mary at Dance holds the most valuable works of the Dubrovnik school of painting

Triptych "Our Lady with Saints", 1517, the last work of master Nikola Božidarević

Polyptich, Lovro Dobričević, 15ᵗʰ C

tourist facilities. Luxurious summer houses were built in Lapad in the 15ᵗʰ and 16ᵗʰ centuries. Especially outstanding is the castle of the Sorkočević family from the 16ᵗʰ C with a large terrace, fishpond, boathouses and a flamboyantly attractive garden. The small votive church of Our Lady of Compassion with a rich collection of the votive paintings of old ships and votive plaques, given by seamen, has been preserved. Also the church of St Michael and its cemetery, the last burial place of Dubrovnik noblemen.

The cross at Srđ, a symbol of pride and defiance of this City ⇨

The Renaissance castle of Petar Sorkočević at Lapad, 16th C

The bridge of Dr. Franjo Tuđman, a miraculous architectonic object that connects two banks of the Rijeka dubrovačka

Performances in front of the Rector's Palace

DUBROVNIK SUMMER FESTIVAL

*T*his is the most significant cultural event in Dubrovnik that has taken place every year from July 10th to August 25th since 1950. During the 45 days of its duration of Dubrovnik becomes an open stage under the stars on which top local and foreign artists perform scenic and musical works by renowned authors both from Croatia and abroad. The opening ceremony takes place in front of the Sponza Palace when the artists symbolically ask the permission of the Rector to enter the City in order to show their skills to the local people. With the sounds of the Hymn to Liberty, the festival flag is hoisted on Orlando's Column where it stays during the entire Festival.

Music revived the Atrium of the Rector's Palace ⇨

MAINLAND AND ISLANDS

ŽUPA DUBROVAČKA

*T*his is an area not too large and within reach of the City of Dubrovnik. In it the material, spiritual and natural heritage has been preserved. Many summer holidays buildings and various remains of different cultures and civilizations which met and influenced each other are found in these areas. The area of Župa Dubrovačka slopes towards the sea like an amphitheatre with the fertile Župsko Polje full of water to irrigate the earth.

Župa dubrovačka, a harmonious whole of the past and present

Picturesque folk costumes of Župa

Župa Dubrovačka has always been in contiguity with the sea and the land. Always in touch with Dubrovnik, this ancient City-State with which for centuries it shared its philosophy of life, and accepted the various historical, political and cultural movements. At the same time it has always remained the authentic Župa Dubrovačka, which was historically known as the Illyrian Brenum and Slavonic Žrnovnica (derived from the millers' craft), and is situated between Dubrovnik and Duboka Ljuta. It still remembers its Greek and Roman times, the strong onslaught of Slav and Avar tribes, Croats, and, of course, the Republic of Dubrovnik with which it was economically and strategically connected, plus the French occupation, and Austro-Hungarian rule.

Župa settlements illustrate both the past and the present leaning both towards the sea and the land.

Kupari, Srebreno, Mlini and Plat are summer resorts with beautiful beaches, clear sea and luxurious Mediterranean vegetation.

Dubac is the first settlement from the direction of Dubrovnik and is known for its special kind of quality stone. Čibača is situated in the very heart Of Župa where Dubrovnik noblemen built summer houses and castles. Zakula, is an old settlement with a picturesque nucleus of stone houses. Then there is Rovanj with the Dominican monastery and the church of St Vicenza and Mandaljena, immersed in a fertile oval shaped valley. The parish church of St Mary Magdalena dominates this settlement and is mentioned in documents of 1285; Gornji and Donji Bragat are frontier settlements that have always been guardians of peace. Postranje with well preserved old rural architecture is a monument of its kind to human labour and skilfulness while Buići abounds in springs of water that irrigated the fertile valley and powered the ancient mills. Lastly there is Petrače, a picturesque settlement on the slopes of sunny Malaštice.

Kupari

This is the oldest settlement in Župa in which the first hotel was built in 1920. Beaches, parks and a pathway are well arranged and kept.

Sports facilities and other amenities for rest and recreation are being built for both summer and winter tourism. All the hotels look attractive from the outside and have various tourist facilities. Kupari gets its name from "Kuparica", a centre for producing tiles ("kupe").

Srebreno

Earlier, this was a peasant and fishermen's village mentioned for the first time in 1272. Today it is a tourist resort with plenty of entertainment, sports and recreation. Dubrovnik noblemen used to build summer houses there.

Mlini

This is an old historical settlement and centre of the milling craft. Water used to come from here to Dubrovnik earlier especially in dry summer months when a big aqueduct was constructed. The parish church of St Ilar is situated in the oldest part of Mlini. According to legend St Illar Christianized the Illyrians here. They were shepherds and were afraid of snakes.

The widespread branches of a plane-tree which was planted in 1743 offer a pleasant and refreshing shade. Mlini has been a resting place and meeting point for generations for the men

Mlini, a tourist resort at Župa dubrovačka

and women of Župa. The rivulet Vrelo flows noisily through Mlini, irrigates the centuries-old plane-tree and then gently flows out to the sea.

The men of Dubrovnik have always looked here as a place for holidays, rest, walking and recreation. Tourism had already begun to develop here in the 19th century when visitors were accommodated in small hotels and villas.

Soline

Soline lies below the Adriatic Road, the Magistrala, next to the sea. The name Soline came because of its salt-works, mentioned in ancient times. Numerous visitors here enjoy very much what it has to offer and frequently return to this place.

Plat

Plat was built at the very end of Župa as the old Belenum, a picturesque settlement with beautiful pebble beaches, clear sea and flagrant vegetation.

Duboka Ljuta

It has been mentioned recently as a Robinson Crusoe cove, to the northeast of the Župa Bay from which the way leads towards Cavtat and Konavle.

Plat, the clean sea, lush vegetation and comfortable hotels

KONAVLE

With its gentle and attractive landscape Konavle has preserved its ancient roots, building heritage and specially beautiful female folk costumes. Various cultures touched this area and various peoples opposed each other leaving permanent and inerasable remains.

There are various assumptions about the origins of Konavle but the most logical one is that the name Konavle derives from *canabula* meaning a canal for bringing water and so reclaiming the fields. Irrigation canals have always been a speciality of Konavle.

Konavle came under the possession of the Republic of Dubrovnik for whom this gentle and rich valley was very important. Konavosko Polje has ideal conditions for the cultivation of vine, especially the famous Dubrovnik Malvasia.

In Konavle one can admire the contrasts of steep hills and fertile fields, coves and beautiful beaches, inaccessible rocks in bays closed in with peninsulas and islets, while inland there are springs and small rivers. This is a rare mixture in such a small area which stretches from Konavle and Duboka Ljuta to the peninsula of Prevlaka at the very end of the Dubrovnik-Neretva County.

Konavle hills and the range of Sniježnica (1,234 metres high) have been centuries-long protectors of Konavle. On this pieace of land, numerous old buildings have been preserved. There are the remains of a Roman aqueduct, a Glagolitic inscription from the 11th C, Roman inscriptions in stone, parts of still-standing tomb-stones, and the early-Croatian little church of St Demetrius in Gabrili.

Today, Konavle is becoming more and more a tourist destination with attractive features. Apart from village tourism, excursions, folklore performances at Čilipi, the Franciscan monastery and Rector's Palace at Pridvorje, there are trips to Kuna Konavoska and Sniježnica, visit to Aesculapius's Cave, a trip up to Konavle's hilly area with a pilgrimage to the cross at Mount Stražišće, the place where an American plane came down in 1996, excursions to Vojski Do, the place where many of the defenders of Konavle were killed, and so a place for paying homage to the Homeland, with a visit to the peninsula of Prevlaka and its monumental fortress-monument - a symbol for protection and a message for peace.

Holidays at Molunat, situated in a beautiful bay, and Cavtat, the favourite of the gods, of nature and of people, are memorable. And there are many other tourist possibilities: jeep-safari, horse riding, cycling, diving, boating, even extreme sports...

There are some thirty villages in Konavle with picturesque backgrounds and authentic village buildings. The villages of Jasenice, Brotnice, Šilješci, Duba, Stravča and Kuna in the Konavle hills have an undisturbed old stone architecture. A typical tomb-stone has been preserved at Brotnice having scenes of shooting, animals, wheels and an inscription in the bosančica script.

Ancient tomb-stones can also be found at Gabrili, Mihanići and Dunave. The village of Gruda has developed along the edge of the fertile Konavosko Polje, as the economic centre of Konavle, while the settlement of Ljuta in the protected area of the River Ljuta is just three kilometres away together with its famous Konavoski dvori, a well-known excursion point and restaurant with local specialities. Dunave, Dubravka and Vodovađa are settlements in the hilly part of Konavle.

The remains of Soko-grad, a monumental frontier fort facing the hinterland of Herzegovina, have also been preserved. From this fort, you get a magnificent view of Konavle. Konavle settlements near the sea are also at Močići where an engraved relief in rock of the god Mithra slaying the bull can be seen; Popovići with its kominate, a unique example of the autochthonous Konavle building art; Radovčići, and Poljice are also very attractive.

Some Illyrian necropolises holding the tombs of their leaders have been carefully preserved in Mikulići and Pločice.

The cypresses at Konavle

Pridvorje

Pridvorje was the seat of the rector of Konavle who lived at this Court built in the 15th century. During the administration of the Republic of Dubrovnik 520 rectors from the ranks of Dubrovnik noblemen were installed in Konavle. Among them poet Ivan Gundulić was twice elected as Rector of Konavle.

Pridvorje, the Franciscan Monastery ⇨
and the church of St Blaise

When Montenegrin soldiers burned down Konavle in 1806 the Court also was heavily damaged and it has remained in ruins until the present day.

The complex of the Franciscan monastery from the 15th C, with the church of St Blaise, is both a sacred and cultural centre of Konavle.

Čilipi

Čilipi expresses the true Konavle identity through its County Museum with exhibits of the Konavle folk costumes, domestic artefacts and jewellery. Traditional folklore dances on Sundays take place regularly in front of the church of St Nicolas and are very attractive for visitors seeing these original Konavle dances, rich folk costumes adorned with gold embroidery and also with some attractive handicrafts stalls.

The village developed on the remains of an old settlement next to the 14th C parish church. Simple white stone houses make Čilipi attractive for both local and foreign visitors.

Sunday folklore performances at Čilipi, enjoying music and dance

CAVTAT

*T*his medieval small town with two peninsulas, Rat and Supetar, enclosing two harbours lies 16 kilometres to the east of Dubrovnik. It has been built over the centuries in a pleasant Mediterranean ambience where the ancient Roman town of Epidaurus once stood. Today it is the administrative, cultural and tourist centre of Konavle.

Epidaurus was destroyed with the invasion of the Avars and Slavs and its inhabitants were forced to move to the neighbouring protected settlement of Laus – later Dubrovnik. Close links between Cavtat and Dubrovnik continued under the administration of the Republic of Dubrovnik in which Cavtat was the second most important town. Many summer houses surrounded by lush gardens were built; also streets. churches, and quays on the water front.

This is a town of gentle beauty, unique heritage, and a place of rest, entertainment, and peace. Cavtat's well-known citizens include the painter Vlaho Bukovac, writer of legal books Baltazar Bogišić, and politician Frano Supilo. Its name is derived from the Latin word *civitas* which illustrates the urban quality of this beautiful town. After the Republic of Dubrovnik purchased the western part of Konavle in 1426, two small towns were built – Cavtat to the west and Molunat to the south. These two towns were of great importance to the Republic because they were able to serve as refuges for the inhabitants of Dubrovnik in case of danger. The Turkish danger was great at that time, so that Molunat became, indeed, a place for refugees, while Cavtat was used for holidays.

The ancient Cavtat, the historical and cultural centre of Konavle

Today, Cavtat is a well developed tourist centre with valuable cultural and historical places of interest. There is the house where the painter Vlaho Bukovac was born, with an atelier and a gallery; while the parish church of St Nicolas houses valuable artefacts. There is the mausoleum of the Račić family, the work of Ivan Meštrović; and the Renaissance Rector's Palace from the 16th C is there. Earlier the seat of the rector and state administration of the Republic of Dubrovnik, it is today a gallery with a collection of works of art, graphics, ethnographic items, numismatic collections and arms. There is the rich library of Baltazar Bogišić with about 20,000 books. The Franciscan monastery, and the church of the celestial female protector of Cavtat, Our Lady of the Snows, houses a rich collection of works of art, the polyptych of St Michael from 1510, the work of the Renaissance painter of the Dubrovnik school of painting, Vicko Lovrin Dobričević. Last, but not least, the Šipun Cave is an attraction for any visitor to Cavtat.

Cavtat, Franciscan Monastery, a detail ⇨
of the Polyptych of St Michael,
the work of Vicko Lovrin Dobričević

RIJEKA DUBROVAČKA

*T*hat is a long bay at the end of which there is the karst spring water of Rijeka Dubrovačka or the Ombla river. Here the water is calm and suitable for fishing and rowing sports. The area of Rijeka Dubrovačka lies between steep rocky hills and has pleasant summer temperatures which was noticed by many noblemen of Dubrovnik so that they decided to build their summer homes there. Among those buildings that survived the changes over the centuries, the most representative is Sorkočević's Summer House not far from the spring and the marina. The settlements of Stara and Nova Mokošica, Komolac, Sustjepan, and Rožat also developed along the banks of the river. Sustjepan is one of the oldest settlements in Rijeka Dubrovačka with the church of St Stephen from the 11th and 12th centuries. Behind Komolac there is the spring of the River Ombla on which a dam and mills were built. In Rožat, one can see the remains of a Benedictine monastery from 1123, abandoned in the 13th C. A Franciscan monastery from 1393 was renovated in 1704.

Rijeka Dubrovačka, full of tourist challenges

Important writers and scribes lived within the walls of the Franciscan Monastery at Rožat

DUBROVAČKO PRIMORJE
(Dubrovnik Littoral)

A picturesque area with beautiful bays, indented coast, and a clear sea. Some attractive villages can be found here, plus the well-known dance linđo performed by young people and accompanied by a "lijerica" (a small violin and bow).

In a large and protected bay there are two villages: Mali Zaton and Veliki Zaton, a favourite excursion point by sea or road from Dubrovnik.

Orašac

Orašac is situated at the foot of Mount Vračevo and Mount Goli and contains the summer house of Filip Saponare from 1700, built in the shape of a tower. Next to it there is what was a Dominican monastery from 1690 with a small church. The 16th C Soderini Castle stands below the village on the edge of a high rock.

Trsteno

One of the most beautiful Dubrovnik villages outstanding for its two giant plane trees which are more than 400 years old. Trsteno also has an arboretum next to the chateaux of the Gučetić family around which there is a park with rare plants. Speaking about Trsteno brings to mind one of the most beautiful of all Dubrovnik women, the magnificent Cvijeta Zuzorić who, in this idyllic ambience, discussed beauty with Maro Gundulić, in a work published in Italian in 1581.

Slano

The name means salty and was given to Slano during the time of the Republic of Dubrovnik when the inhabitants of this village smuggled salt from the Ston salt-works. Salt, at that time, was a precious and expensive commodity. This area was already inhabited in prehistory. This can be seen from the remains of hill-forts in the nearby hills. The remains of a Roman castrum have been preserved as well as early Christian sarcophagi. Slano has beautiful beaches, dense woods and walks along by the sea.

Slano, a picturesque hamlet on the Dubrovnik coast

The Mali Ston bay and its islets

⇦ *Neputn's Fountain in the garden of the summer house of the Gučetić family at Trsteno*

ISLANDS

ISLAND OF LOKRUM

*L*okrum has always been very closely connected with the history of Dubrovnik. Owing to its geographic position, it was a military and strategic support for the protection of the city harbour both against the destructive force of the sea and from enemy attacks thus preventing any sudden assault. Lokrum first entered the history of Dubrovnik when the City donated it to the Benedictines who built a monastery and a church on it. Although the island enjoyed a certain religious autonomy, it was still a consistent part of the Dubrovnik administrative area.

The previous Benedictine monastery on the island of Lopud near Dubrovnik

The monastery was abolished in 1798 and the possessions of the Benedictines were sold. It was bought later by the Habsburgs in 1859 and became the summer residence of this Austrian dynasty. Today, Lokrum is protected as a "reserve of special woods and vegetation". The whole island is full of pine and laurel trees, "a garden on the sea" and the most visited Dubrovnik beach. During the summer months Lokrum is daily connected with the city by small boats. One can enjoy swimming here, and also walking through the dense pine woods and the park which is rich in sub-tropical vegetation. Especially interesting is the so called Dead Sea, a small lake in the middle of the island.

ELAPHITE ISLANDS

Within reach of Dubrovnik, there are seven islands known as the Elaphite Islands: Daksa, Koločep, Sveti Andrija, Lopud, Rude, Šipan, and Jakljan. The name derives from the Greek word "elafos" meaning deer.

Daksa

Daks is the first islet after leaving the harbour of Gruž and the smallest Elaphite island. This uninhabited islet in the form of a crescent is covered with pine trees, cypresses, carobs, cactuses, lemon and orange trees.

Koločep

The first bigger inhabited island in the immediate vicinity of Dubrovnik is Koločep. There are two villages on it: Gornje Čelo and Donje Čelo. The island is of limestone and there are no springs of drinkable water here. It is covered with Mediterranean vegetation. The highest peak on the island is Križ, 125 metres above sea level. After the arrival of the Croats to the Adriatic it came within the administration of Travunija, and after the 9thC under the Republic of Dubrovnik. It is mentioned in old documents under the name of Calaphota or Calamota, while the Statute of Dubrovnik already mentions the island in 1272. An important branch of the Koločep economy from the 14th to the 17th centuries was coral diving. The divers of Koločep used to pick up coral not only around their island, where rich deposits existed, but also along the whole of the Adriatic, the Aegean Sea and around Malta.

Koločep is a favourite excursion for point Dubrovnik people and for tourists due to its beautiful beaches, clear sea and flagrant vegetation.

Sveti Andrija

This is an uninhabited isolated islet west of Dubrovnik swept by wind and washed by the sea. It was first inhabited by the Benedictines who built a monastery and the church of St Andrew, because of which the islet received its name. The Dubrovnik poet Mavro Vetranović lived here as a hermit in the middle of the 16th century. In his poem 'Remeta', he vividly described the storms and his modest Mediterranean vegetative diet.

Lopud

The most developed Elaphite island with village of the same name. This is an island of rich history and valuable cultural heritage. It is covered with dense Mediterranean vegetation - olive groves, vineyards and plantations of citrus

Croatian chapels and 24 others are scattered across the island.

Above the beautiful cove of Šunj with its sandy beach 800 metres long, the church of Our Lady of Šunj rises. It was built in the 15th C and holds valuable paintings.

The richest man of all times from Lopud was definitely Miho Pracat, the ship-owner and merchant who had no heirs and so left in his will all his riches to the Republic of Dubrovnik to be used for humanitarian purposes.

A nice love story from the 17th century *Marija from Lopud* is connected with this island. It relates the unhappy love affair of a poor young girl Marija and a young nobleman called Lujo.

Šipan

Šipan is the largest Elaphite island with two villages, Šipanska Luka and Suđurađ between which the fertile Šipansko Polje extends with numerous vineyards and olive groves. The island is surrounded with picturesque uninhabited islets, rocks and reefs. It was mentioned for the first time under its present name in 1371. Some remains from prehistory have been preserved, and also from Roman and Byzantine times, and there are early-Croatian churches and chapels. The Renaissance Rector's Court from the time of the Dubrovnik Republic in Šipanska Luka has a beautiful view of the whole bay, land, and islets. Also preserved are some summer homes of owned by the noblemen of Dubrovnik. The fortified Renaissance 16th C summer house of the Tjepović-Skočibuha family has also been well preserved. Antun Paskoje Kazali (1815-1894), an erudite linguist, and well-known expert on Shakespeare lived here in his old age.

Lopud, an island of mild climate and lush Mediterranean vegetation

fruits. In ancient times it was known under the name Delaphodia, and then under the Roman form of Lafota. Since the 11th C it became within the Republic of Dubrovnik, and since 1457 the seat of a princedom, when a Rector's Palace started to be built. In the 16th C it had its own fleet of some eighty ships, as well as a shipyard. Rich seamen built luxurious houses, arranged the village, while noblemen and merchants of Dubrovnik built their summer houses there, surrounding them with gardens and parks. Two monasteries, one Dominican from 1482 and the other Franciscan from 1483, plus four early

Donje Čelo lies in a protected cove to the northwest of the island of Koločep

The hamlet of Šipanska Luka lies on the southwest side of the island of Šipan

THE ISLAND OF MLJET

A poet said that the beauty of nature was created here better than all human skill could achieve. Mljet is one of our most beautiful islands full of lush Mediterranean vegetation growing in a gentle ambience. It is known for its dense pine woods reaching to the very sea shore, its indented coast, beautiful sandy beaches and a unique natural phenomenon – a Big and a Smaller Lake in the middle of the island. The folk costumes of Mljet are also attractive.

According to legend Mljet is the island where the nymph Calypso received Odysseus on his way back after the fall of Troy. Odysseus was so enchanted by Calypso and her magical island that he stayed, it is said, for several years.

Due to the unique beauty of the landscape, with its centuries-old Mediterranean woods of holm-oak and pine, the canals of Soline, the Big and Smaller Lake, and its cultural and historical heritage that includes ancient palaces, the early-Christian basilica at Polače, the Benedictine monastery from the 12th C on the islet of St Mary, and also due to the people who have lived here from ancient times, the northwest area of Mljet was proclaimed a National Park.

The island has been well-known since ancient times for its olive oil and good wine.

The Benedictine Monastery was built on the tiny island of St Mary and its church is an outstanding example of Romanesque building.

This islet was for centuries the residence of famous men including some poets, mostly Dubrovnik noblemen, who enjoyed the peace and quiet when creating their literary works. It is mentioned in the past under the names of Melita, Melata, Melta, Malta, and Melad. The oldest sources that mention Mljet are connected with Greek authors from the 4th century B.C. This island is an absolute treasury of cultural and historical heritage from the Illyrian hill-forts to the Greek, Roman and medieval buildings. The remains of the ancient palace at Polače and the early Christian basilica are the island's most valuable buildings, while a palace from Roman times is among the most memorable buildings on our coast.

In the largest and oldest village on the island, Babino Polje, situated in the very middle of the island, the Rector's Palace from the 15th C has been preserved, as well as Sotnica, the court, and administrative buildings and manor houses from the 15th C and summer houses from the time of the Republic of Dubrovnik.

The following villages were developed under the dense green coves of trees: Pomena, the tourist centre of the island; Goveđari and Babine Kuće on the banks of the Big Lake; Soline, named because of the production of salt organized by the Benedictines, and, Blato, a village in the middle of the island next to a large farming area. Sobra is a maritime traffic centre on the island; while Prožura is an old medieval settlement built around the church of St Trinity and the monastery from the 15th C. Then there is Prožurska Luka, a fishermen's and tourist village; Maranovići, an old settlement with spacious olive groves; Okuklje, a protected harbour and the favourite anchorage of sailors, and Korita, named after the stone troughs which are filled with water during rainy periods from a small spring; and the cove of Saplunara with its beautiful sandy beaches surrounded with pine trees. So it is easy to see why Mljet, this green jewel, is becoming more and more attractive as a tourist destination.

⇐ *The island of Mljet, the islet of St Mary emerged from the sea in the middle of the Big Lake*

PENINSULA OF PELJEŠAC

*T*he Peninsula is long and mountainous extending between the Neretva River and Mali Ston bays from the north and east, and the Mljet and Pelješac channels from the south and west. Pelješac is the only Dalmatian peninsula and is rich materially, spiritually and in its natural heritage. This peninsula was first settled by the Illyrians, then the Greeks and Romans. It came under the Republic of Dubrovnik for five and a half centuries which made full use of its natural salt beds.

The massive Peninsula has a long maritime tradition as region of seamen and sea captains, well-known for their skill and courage.

It has also been the cradle of wine-growing from ancient times. Especially known are its red wines Dingač, Postup and Mali Plavac. The Mali Ston Bay, between the peninsula and the mainland has long been an ideal place for cultivating oysters, mussels and other shell fish. Ston oysters are among the best in Europe; they are a rare sort of sea shell that has remained autochthonous and unchanged, resistant to disease. Ston menus are also abundant in gastronomic specialities from various sea foods prepared with the virgin olive oil from the area and seasoned with aromatic herbs.

Pelješac is divided into four communities: Ston, Janjina, Orebić and Trpanj. All its towns and villages bear the marks of bygone centuries. There is the picturesque cove of Prapratno with its ancient olive trees and a large sandy beach; the idyllic Žuljana; the fishermen's settlement of Drače; Janjina as one of the oldest Pelješac small towns surrounded with fertile vineyards and olive groves is where noblemen of Dubrovnik built beautiful houses such as the Getaldić house, the house of princely administration with the figure of St Blaise; Sreser with its vineyards in the background, and the ferry port of Trstenik; Kuna, stretching along a fertile valley, is the birth place of the Croatian painter Mato Celestin Medović and is known for its monastery and the church of Dolorita, a place of pilgrimage; Crkvice on the northern side of the peninsula; Potomje known for its high quality wines; Trpanj, a tourist destination and ferry-port on the northeast coast of Pelješac with its dense Mediterranean vegetation and old Renaissance mansions. The Baroque church of Our Lady of Carmel was built in the 17th century while its bell-tower with the clock was added later. Kučište and Viganj abound with elegant houses of the old sea captains; and, not forgetting the pastoral hamlet of Nakovane and Lovište, the youngest Pelješac village and now a tourist destination.

STON

*S*ton is a remarkable town with one of the longest medieval defensive walls in Europe, built according to previous plans in the 14th century. This is a town of narrow streets, old elegant houses, a town of salt-works and the preserved remains of old cultures. When this town, 65 kilometres away from Dubrovnik, came under the Republic of Dubrovnik in 1333, two connecting small towns were formed, Veliki Ston and Mali Ston with three huge fortifications: Veliki Kaštio, Koruna and Podzvizd. The walls be-

Ston, a small medieval town fortified with walls with salt works dating from the time of the Dubrovnik Republic

tween the fortresses are 5 kilometres long and they were built, rebuilt and additionally added to from the 14th to the 16th centuries. These city walls, "the European Chinese Wall", were the safest of guardians for the simple reason that nobody could approach the peninsula without being seen.

Mali Ston is situated on the north side of the peninsula under the Koruna Fortress which, with its four towers, looks like a crown. The round tower of Toljevac from 1491 is unique in this part of the world.

Historically the more important Ston was the second town of the Republic of Dubrovnik because of both its size and its importance to the Republic. Ston is interwoven with signifi-

Mali Ston, a picturesque small town well-known by high-quality Oysters

Trpanj, a tourist resort on the northeast coast of the peninsula of Pelješac

cant buildings which are incorporated into the defensive system of the town and its surroundings. The most important are: the Rector's Palace, the church of St Blaise, the loggia of the city guards, the Renaissance Bishop's Palace with the portico from the 16th C, the Franciscan monastery with Gothic-Renaissance cloisters and the church of St Nicholas which holds the crucifixion by Blaž Jurjev Trogiranin from 1428. On the top of the hill Gradac, not far from Ston, there is the pre-Romanesque church of St Michael from the 11th C.

The salt-works of Stone are among the oldest in Europe, and even today salt is produced in the natural way. The technology in the production of these white salt crystals has not changed since ancient times only following the natural sequence of picking up the salt when the north wind, the "bura", blows and when there is strong hot sunshine.

Orebić, the town of famous sea captains and of a long maritime tradition

OREBIĆ

Orebić is an ancient small town on the south coast of the Pelješac peninsula facing Korčula. It is a strongly maritime town with beautiful old sea captains' houses surrounded with gardens full of exotic plants brought back from overseas and Mediterranean vegetation. The long maritime history of this town can be seen in its Maritime Museum. Orebić experienced its full growth and development with the Republic of Dubrovnik. The road leads up from Orebić towards the higher parts of the peninsula and to the Renaissance Franciscan monastery with its cloisters and the Gothic church of Our Lady of the Assumption. It had both a religious and strategic role because it was situated at the border between the Republic of Dubrovnik and Venice, which always presented a potential menace to the Republic. The little monastery is

The Franciscan Monastery above Orebić, built in 1470, holds exceptional artefacts

a treasury of various artefacts; especially valuable are two marble bas-reliefs of Our Lady with the Son, the work of Renaissance masters and the statue of Christ on the Cross made by Juraj Petrović in 1458. For Orebić's seamen it was a shrine, so that it holds a collection of votive gifts from grateful sailors. From the monastery's belvedere a magnificent view extends over the Pelješac Channel, the Korčula Archipelago, and further.

This did not pass unnoticed in the writings of outstanding English travel writers from the beginning of the 20th century.

Today Orebić is a developed tourist destination with modern hotels, campsites, beautiful small pebble beaches, rich folklore tradition (especially its famous "Captains' Dance"), various cultural and entertainment events, and interesting excursions.

THE ISLAND OF KORČULA

Korčula is one of the largest and most inhabited islands in the Croatian Adriatic Sea. It has been covered with dense pine woods from ancient times so that the Greek colonists named it Korkyra Melaina (Black Korčula). The forests of the island have provided the material for the construction of wooden ships and boats so that Korčula shipbuilders became well known all over the world for their craft. In the 16th and 17th centuries, they constructed each year between 500 and 700 ships, both small and big for the transport of various cargos and

for fishing. Korčula was also known for its first quality stone, especially from the islet of Vrnik and it was used to build not only the luxurious mansions of Dalmatian towns, but also well-known buildings all over the world including the basilica of St Sophia in Constantinople, the parliament in Vienna, the town hall in Stockholm, etc. The town of Korčula was built from the same stone and produced in numerous stone-cutting workshops on the island. This tradition of building was passed down from generation to generation.

Korčula, the old town ⇨

The interior of the cathedral of St Mark with the ciborium (baldachin), the work of Marko Andrijić, 1486

THE TOWN OF KORČULA

The men of Korčula are also well known as cultivators of olive trees, and as winemakers and fishermen. The wines of Korčula were already produced in ancient times, while the wine areas around Blato, Lumbarda, the fields of Čara and Smokvica have long been on all the wine maps of the world. The most famous Korčula white wines are Grk, Pošip and Rukatac.

The oldest island settlements developed in the interior of the island: Žrnovo, Pupnat, Čara, Smokvica and Blato, while only the town of Korčula was built on the sea. Lumbarda, Račišće and Vela Luka were only developed later.

Korčula Town lies at the northeast end of the island on a point of the indented coast. The old Korčula town, surrounded by its city walls is one of the best preserved towns of Adriatic heritage building. The early presence of the Greeks and later Romans in Korčula was of great influence in further developing the town and laid the grounds for an early medieval town after the arrival of the Croats in the 7th and 8th centuries.

In the 15th and 16th centuries stone-cutting workshops were founded and the skill of processing and sculpting stone is evident on the façades of Korčula houses, balconies, portals, windows, and coats-of-arms. The Korčula stone masons passed on their skills even outside their own town. The most important Korčula stone masons came from the Andrijić family who produced top quality stone masons from the 14th century onwards. Among many beautiful churches and mansions, one of the most beautiful is the Gabrielis Palace on the main city square which is dominated by the cathedral of St Mark from the 15th C. It was built by local masters using the hard white Korčula stone. Opposite the cathedral there is the elegant Arneri Palace, while the Bishop's Court is situated next to the cathedral. It houses the Abbatial Treasury, a precious collection of church artefacts and valuable documents of church and town history. Especially precious are the polyptych by Blaž Jurjev Trogiranin from the 15th C and Ugrinović's Madonna from the 14th C, together with many original paintings by both Dalmatian and Italian masters. There are also gold and silver chalices, crosses, rare parchments from the 12th C, and various religious books. The paintings by Italian Renaissance masters, portraits of Korčula bishops and abbots, old chasubles, and the works of modern Korčula and Croatian painters and sculptors, all tell of the high taste of Korčula people.

The House of Marko Polo is a late-Gothic ruin with a square tower. According to legend Marko Polo was born in a previous house at the same place.

The bell-tower of the cathedral church of St Mark – like a dream in stone

Korčula has continued the tradition of the sword dance Moreška from the 16th century.

Korčula Towns and Villages

Lumbarda has spread itself out on the eastern end of the island and on the surrounding hills and is remarkable for its vineyards of a special sort of vine Grk. A Greek colony was founded here in the 3rd century B.C.. It was in the 16th century that the rich people of Korčula built their fortified homes and summer houses in Lumbarda, which is only 6 kilometres away from Korčula. Well-known are the mansions of the Nobilo family, and the Milina and Kršinić families.

Korčula, the church of All Saints, Blaž Jurjev Trogiranin, the Polyptych of All Saints, 16th C

The inhabitants of Lumbarda mostly occupy themselves with wine-growing, fishing and stone-cutting and, these days of course, tourism.

Further on, towards the interior of the island, there is the village of Žrnovo mentioned in documents of the Middle Ages. Žrnovo has maintained the tradition of performing the sword dance Moštra which is still performed. Pupnat is another village with the tradition of performing the knightly dance with long swords called Kumpanjija. Pupnat, the highest village, has its own harbour, Pupnatska luka, down on the sea. Čara is an old village of winegrowers producing the high quality wine Pošip, and also the tradition of performing the Kumpanjija. In Čarsko Polje, in the middle of the vineyards there is the votive church of Our Lady of the Field of Čara form the 14th C., the central pilgrimage shrine of the island of Korčula. Zavalatica, nearby Čara at sea level, is full of modern family houses, built by the people of Čara and by overseas emigrants. Smokvica also produces Pošip from its rich vineyards in Smokvičko Polje. Going south from Smokvica towards the sea one arrives at Brna, a beautiful bay rich in pine trees. Inland again and going west, Blato, a small town but important as a business centre, is noted for its long alley of elm trees and the three-aisled church of All Saints. The chapel of St Vicenza, the protector saint of Blato, was added in the 18th C. The solemn sword dance Kumpanjija is performed here on her feast-day. Vela Luka is the largest town on the island

The bell-tower of the cathedral of St Mark dominates the Korčula roofs

and was developed at the beginning of the 19th C. It is well-known both in Croatia and abroad for its spa "Kalos" for rheumatic diseases and rehabilitation. Vela Luka has numerous coves ideal for swimming and a very attractive woody islet, Ošjak. Račišće, 14 kilometres away from the town of, is a fishermen's village with a very good natural protected harbour (and facing north on the island) and the native home of skilful seamen.

*The chivalrous play Moreška, a unique sword dance ⇨
performed in Korčula only*

THE ISLAND OF LASTOVO

*T*his is the Croatia's most southernmost inhabited island. Its shores are steep, but there are also sandy bays such as Ubli, Skrivena luka and Zaklopatica. The highest peak on the island is Mount Hum (417 metres). The greater part of the island is covered with macchis, while the slopes of the hills are rich in pine trees and Mediterranean oak. Together with Mljet, Lastovo is Croatia's most woody island due to the forestry policy of the Republic of Dubrovnik.

Although the earliest traces of life on the island reach as early as the Bronze Age, this island of wine and olive-growers was first mentioned as a Greek colony in the Adriatic, under the name of Ladesta, Ladeston and Ladestris. A larger settlement existed on the western coast of the island in Roman times. It was in the possession of Byzantium in the early Middle Ages, and since the 9th C was under the Neretljani; Venice occupied it in the 10th century, and, in the 11th and 12th centuries it belonged to Zahumlje, and later to the Republic of Dubrovnik. The French established their authority on the island between 1808 and 1813 under Napoleon and the Austro-Hungarian Empire took over from 1815 to 1918. Under the Treaty of Rapallo of 1920, Lastovo belonged to Italy and it stayed under Italian rule until 1943, when, and after the end of the Second World War in 1945, it became part of the Federal People's Republic of Yugoslavia.

Lastovo, an island washed in the blue sea with a centuries-long history

The Dubrovnik Republic has left here the deepest marks both in its organization of the administration and in the overall economy. The medieval Statute of Lastovo of 1310 with its regulations and written customs is an important document for studying the history of Lastovo. There are two settlements on the island that have a long history, Lastovo and Ubli. The entire island is a paradise for boatmen, while an excellent choice of fish and various sea foods prepared in the traditional using high quality olive oil and good wine are a real treat for gourmets. The island of Lastovo is surrounded by no less than 46 islets around which various sorts of fish attract the fishermen. It is a special island for quiet holidays and the enjoyment of clear sea, hidden coves, paths for cyclists and walkers. There is one road that crosses the island.

The town of Lastovo was built high up like an amphitheatre facing towards the interior of the island and not towards the sea. It boasts old stone houses and unique and unusual chimneys – "fumari" - following the architectonic fash-ion of the 17th and 18th centuries. Dubrovnik and Korčula stone masters between them built the parish church of St Cosmas and Damion in the 15th C. Lastovo has 46 churches and chapels among which the oldest is the small church of St Luke from the 11th C, while the most beautiful one is the Gothic-Renaissance church of St Mary in the Field from the 15th C, with the precious altar painting of Our Lady with the Child Jesus - the work of the Venetian painter Francesco Bissolo. There are also 46 cultivated farming areas and hilltops and valleys, 46 islands, islets and rocks in the archipelago, while the area of Lastovo also has 46 square kilometres.

Lastovo has especially rich folk costumes, and there is a tradition of old dances and habits. Especially interesting are the Carnival festivities, the famous Lastovo Poklad, unique in the world.

The underwater world around Lastovo is fascinating and it is a delight to dive around Lastovnjaci and Vrhovnjaci, and the islet of Glavat on which stands a lighthouse. This is situated to the east of Lastovo, and the island of Sušac to the west.

THE VALLEY OF THE NERETVA RIVER

God and nature were both generous towards the valley of the Neretva River. They gave it beauty and an interesting history, authenticity and tradition, an abundance of sunshine and water, hard-working and hospitable people. The region of Donja Neretva has more than 3700 sunny hours a year, and a mild and pleasant Mediterranean climate. The entire area was once an enormous swampy space with an abundance of birds and shallow water fish. When it was reclaimed it took on a completely new appearance. Today, orchards and vegetable farms, especially plantations of mandarins cover it in all directions.

The whole region is rich in flora and fauna so that five ichthyologic and ornithological reserves have been established with two protected landscapes, one parklike wood and 26 protected sites. This area is a habitat and winter refuge for two thirds of species of European birds so that it has been proclaimed a wet area of international importance. These natural characteristics of the environment, large swampy areas and their rich vegetative and animal world are the basis for excursion tourism. Sailing through the delta of the Neretva in small long boats (trupice) is an unforgettable experience.

Metković, the marathon boat race on the Neretva River

METKOVIĆ

*M*etković is one of the oldest towns of Donja Neretva (The Lower Neretva). It was first mentioned in historical documents in 1422 and obtained a greater importance after 1715 when the Venetians built here the Neretva harbour. Fast economic development began in the middle of the 19th century when Metković was the most important Dalmatian harbour with a railway connection from 1855. Since 1854 it was the administrative, judicial, tax-collecting and economic centre of Donja Neretva. Its strategic position and movement facilities (harbour, railway, roads) were an important factor in its development. Trade and traffic became the pillars of its economic growth. Later, agriculture also became important.

Today, Metković is the largest town of Donja Neretva. It is situated on the Neretva River, which is navigable as far as Metković, and it is 19 kilometres away from the sea, next to the border with Bosnia and Herzegovina.

Of special value in Metković is the Ornithological collection of 348 different species of stuffed birds. This is among the largest and

A unique attraction – the marathon boat race on the Neretva

richest collections in Europe. The hospitable people of Metković welcome all visitors who can enjoy the beauty of the landscape, cultural and sports events and good cuisine.

The Ancient Town of Narona

The heritage of ancient times gives this region a special value. The most outstanding are the remains of Narona, which except for Salona is the largest ancient town on the eastern Adriatic coast. The remains of Narona can be visited in the village of Vid, 3 kilometres away from Metković. The first archaeological investigations began at the beginning of the 20th century.

Karl Patsch wrote and published in Vienna the first monograph about Narona in 1907. After the Second World War, research work continued under the supervision of experts from the Archaeological Museum in Split, and they were increased in 1988. Narona was a Roman colony which based its richness on trade and represents one of the most precious to remain in the historical heritage of Croatia. When the Augusteum, the temple devoted to Emperor Augustus was discovered this location became the most significant archaeological site outside Rome. Some of the rich treasury from Narona is kept in the Archaeological collection at Vid.

Vid, the stone fragments from ancient Narona

Opuzen, the Neretva River determined the destiny of this town

The man has harnessed the Neretva, the land was intersected with canals and a fertile valley was created

OPUZEN

*T*his small town of Opuzen on the left bank of the Neretva River has its economic basis in agriculture, vegetable producing, fruit growing (sub-tropical fruit, mandarins, figs, etc), and the processing of fruit and vegetables; also fish from the Neretva, and its canals and in the delta lakes. It was mentioned in the Middle Ages under the name of Posrednica. In the 15th century it was a market town of the Republic of Dubrovnik (burned down in 1472). Also in the 15thC the Koš Fortress was built, and in 1865, the Venetians erected Fort Opus at the same place. Opuzen is frequented by numerous visitors who stay on the Adriatic coast and also by sporting fishermen due to the Neretva River being a real challenge to anglers owing to the abundance of various species of fish.

A challenge for fishermen

The blue-brown mosaic of the Neretva valley

PLOČE

*P*loče is the youngest town on the Adriatic coast, and after Rijeka, the largest cargo harbour in Croatia. It is situated a few kilometres to the west of the estuary of the Neretva River, where the plains of its delta and its hilly karst regions meet. Ploče lies at the starting point of the centuries-old natural route up the valley of the Neretva River, connecting the central parts of Bosnia and Herzegovina with the Adriatic Sea. Not far from Ploče are Baćinska jezera (Baćina Lakes), situated next to the spurs of the Biokovo mountain massif. Ploče is connected by ferry with Trpanj on the peninsula of Pelješac.

Baćinska jezera (the Lakes of Baćina), a jewel of nature ⇨

Ploče, a middle Dalmatian port in a deeply protected bay

THE HARMONIOUSNESS OF DUBROVNIK

*G*etting along peacefully with each other or, in other words, civilized behaviour is a special virtue attributed to the men and women of Dubrovnik and their City. This characteristic of Dubrovnik people has been an integral part of their culture of living and dwelling together for centuries. HARMONY, such a nice and simple word, but also an innate virtue, is something that the City gives to every inhabitant at his or her birth.

Luko Paljetak wrote: *Harmoniousness, a category that is aesthetic and ethical, a face but also a mask; this is the way the City shapes its inhabitants – a small bunch of flowers and a small bunch of sprouts, Maro and Baro on the bell-tower, both Green Men, all streets, and one Stradun, that of the mirrors…*

Dubrovnik, the old city port